Jubilate Messi

some poems about football

Steve Ely

Shearsman Books

First published in the United Kingdom in 2018 by
Shearsman Books
50 Westons Hill Drive
Emersons Green
BRISTOL
BS16 7DF

Shearsman Books Ltd Registered Office
30–31 St. James Place, Mangotsfield, Bristol BS16 9JB
(this address not for correspondence)

www.shearsman.com

ISBN 978-1-84861-613-4

Contents

Tohuwabohu

Goddess ex nihilo   burlesquing naked
    from tohuwabohu
parthenogenetic hush-lipped logos
    waltz-whelping wind
wave and welkin   wyrm
    womb-whelmed son-serpent
sperming   the fat-papped
    snake-hipped shekinah   Iahu
        exalted dove

What came first
    the streptopeliac platform of bitten off birch-twigs
bobbing on brine of cosmic amnion
    or the egg
black-winged Night on brooding waters   (some say)
    or sevenfold coils of nachash
proleptic imago   of the male
    red-necked phalarope
brood patch hotter   than Big Bang's blood
    Word's hammering egg-tooth   birth-breaking
chrysalic-empyrean   naming   nidifugous
    night   day   firmament   waters   land
    grass   lights   fowls   whales   cattle
    Man   formed from dirtblood
Hawwah   Mother of All-Living
    (save those that lived before)   *but*

On boreal flat-field   lit by star-spurt creaming cosmos
cropped grass-glade   fenced with knife-skinned aspens
gleaming gainst the viridescence   leathern egg
of pterandon   aepyornis or moa
percnopterus rondo breaking with stones
the blonde head of Jehovah
throne down   by Eden's Angel

Shadow and brawling
the billioned clamour   of ectopistes migratorius
jewelled splintring aspens   pearls
far bigger than pigeons' eggs
cast before condemned   swine

Go forth   lone blackbird
multipliferous   whistling
homely dunnock   go forth in motley

Aspens detonate
and Spirit descending

Fiery Pramanath
explodes with ball
            and roaring

Football in Crowe Street, 1721

Daybreak, Bartlemy Fair. Inns trashed
with Saint's-Eve flotsam; butchers, haberdashers,
poet-suckers, punks, the wits and whimsies
of unwashed Wen, wasted on bottle-ale,
neat jenever. Slum-Lords sotted on malmsey
and sack, lap-lounging, quim-queasy queans.
Gross Chanticleer trumpeting wilted streets,
Goose, Cock, Crowe: time to get up.
Rude rhythm of tabor and cat-call of drum,
trestle-top trap-dancing pattens; two powdered
and periwigged toothless drabs burlesquing
Bent Bob and his Sour Kraut King. The German
presents, the Englishman enters. *A revel!*
No Justice, no Peace; Slack Alice, Moll Quicksheet,
bowing bare-cheeked and exiting Pye-wards,
showered in glistening nobbins.
Drunk soldiery pouring from gin mills
assemble; on rough-field from Bart Church
to Clerkenwell gate, sun shines on the liveried
golden boys swarming the piss-pocket, guttersnipe
streets; haberdashers, butchers and joiners-to-chaos –
cut-purses, apprentice-boys, pimps
and proud beggars – pacing and prowling,
restless for riot.
Sun-flash cleaver – howl and blood-splash
Red Sea parting; skull-hacked haberdash,
nimbused in claret; stretchered from market
to Giltspur's gutter – out-of-bounds. Then tempting fate
from the plank of the scaffold, Jock Chartres
announcing Sally-from-our-Alley, the ball-bearing
bully-off mistress of game. Mob surgent
and brawling – tart tumbled from table,
bow-legged and loose from a half-score of Lords,
ball slipping her skirts like a rabbit – *game on!*

Some shark-mouthed butcher-boy boots the ball skyward;
field follows stampeding like Dungeness beef-kine,
hard-hoofed hobnails rattling cobbles, storm-surge roar
and shattering shingle on Smithfield's slaughterhouse streets.

Ball flies from Crowe   to St. John's Lane
cries up   ball under   herd wheels   and sucks
     to scrummaging vortex   shoulder-to-shoulder
               head down   grappling
     in maelstrom   ball
up someone's jumper   but
     aproned-pit-dogs   ploughshare through
                    fist-down
                    trample
               snotsplash snapteeth
                    howl murder   cry
                              that ball —

          Shark-mouthed butcher-boy
rolling from tumult   leapt hacks
                         duckt forearms
                              swerved
headlocks and nelsons   *catch me if you can*
smashed gutterwards screaming   cannonball blindside —

Ball spurts from the ruck
          open door of the coffee-house
where windows went through
          and tables went over
gentil-men scalded   books broken
                         specs trampled
haymakers   head-butts
guffaw and rawping
          and —

                    Shark-mouthed butcher-boy
racing away
      vaulting trips
          fending side-swipes
              and wrenching free
                  from outstretched arms
                      and grasping fingers
John-Gate's goalhole
      arching before him   spring
          leap like a leopard
              straining for
                              glory –

          Shark-mouthed butcher-boy
rickety
chancred
      fleet as a greyhound   brave as a bear
wrecked sudden
on streetlight
piled frenzy of wolves
      back and forth
      back and forth
      scrum and brawl   back and forth
                              all day
                              with broke jaws
chawing   and gouging
split lips and   shiners
snapped forearms   and shinbones
knotskulls and   crackribs
shivvings   and coshings
          backforth
from Bart-Gate   to goalied St. John's
      when –

Shark-mouthed butcher-boy
    pride of Crowe Street
squirmed from the melee
    with ball at his feet

Shrugged off the maulers
    and rakers of ruck
and dribbled for glory
    out of blood and the muck

Dropped-shoulder step-over
    drag-back and feint
he stooped like a hawk
    on the gate of the Saint

Nutmegged the gaoler
    left him flat on his arse
and smashed the pig's bladder
    through Clerkenwell Arch.

Sunrise, the Feast of St. Austin: up the workers.
Face like raw liver. Bones bruised and buckled,
a nag to the knackers. Bonce banging with beer –
and the ague and the plague and the pox
and the stocks; I've been better. Ten thousand
ways to die. One way to live. Sleeping beside me,
Sally-from-our-Alley, lauded and lorded.
Bit 'o rough. That fucking cockerel.
Time to get up. Still clutching the ball.

British Bulldog

Burntwood Junior & Infants, summer 1973

Who do you want?
Who do you want?

They choose YOU   because they have no choice
so you run   because you have no choice
        bearing down   on the fat kid
the wheezy asthmatic   tinribs
        oyster-face   hole-in-the-heart
elbows   and hand-offs
        shoulder-barge   trampling
swerving strategic   from Nutter   Big Daddy
        but zeroing in   on Shufflebum Baker
whose concrete   flat-back   rifle-crack
        skull-smack   sends dinnertime wheeling
for matron with iodine   invalid carriage
        as you break   the chalked baseline
with a champion's salute
                              BRITISH BULLDOG!

EXPLODE   Wakey and Whitey
        Bucky and Tez   Huffy and Stoppy
Linnit and Nez   Crooksy in calipers
        and Studdy   a lass
escaped from the Colditz   of the so-called Top Class

Who do you want?
Who do you want?

In Cloisters

Deo dante dedi

Gownboys v. Saunderites, fags flanking the scrimmage, sixth-form swankers hooking and striking, breaking and dribbling for Green: smacked-down in Briars, rucked under maul; *shove ye gowneboys, shove! go itte ye cripples!* An hour against the brickwork, shirts shredded and shiners, fags fetching lemons from Green: sometimes scoring.

One-a-side cuppys with Wally and Gaz: up to two, loser int nets. Alternative version; five minutes per match, F.A. Cup from third-round to final; results recorded in Silvine notebook. Keeper as commentator, copying Motson: '*...still Currie... what about that! A quality goal by a quality player...*'

Gateholes, Exley's and Walton's: a tennisy, more often than not. Up to twenty, each man his own mic: *there goes the whistle and it's Leeds twenty, Juventus sixteen, Sniffer Clarke with a quintuple hat-trick.*

Sometimes lasses: hot-rice bounce-twice or corsey-edges, chalk-base rounders and dustbin cricket. And sometime ball less; Bull-dog from Goacher's to Stan Peart's lampost, pie-crust pile-on, Titsy Tyrell.

One kick – playing for snookers off Mitchell's fence, Smeg daubed *LUFC*. Pass-and-shoot into Cotterill's privet, Stu Downs' ineptitude a proxy for Sprake; *Careless Hands*. Twitching nets and hammering window: *get off our part and get back to your own!* Urchin repartee: *it int your part, it's council's!* Two-bob swervers bost in branches, Frank Cotterill's knifing rose-beds.

Best ball caseys for game on green. Crossbars, penalties, fouling soccer: pick sides. *I pee. I po. I'm the man. Pick who you can.* And the big one, Wimpy Wanderers v. Park Estate Pirates: eleven, twelve, two-dozen-a-side, box-to-box til Batty Bat came out.

Ronnie walking their Brandy, street-scouting for Boysy: round-neck, heavy-cotton, royal-blue jerseys, tie-ups and Simlam Stri-kers. Association Rules, Charterhouse, '63. The Green Game, of sorts; runabout, shootabout, puntabout, barging. No skidding in dogshit, booby-trap kerbstones, corsey-coal, skip-ropes, Danny Oates ices – Clock Row's corner-flagged, marked-out arena, where Benny notched nine against Bentley Green Imps and Coco saved three pens – dreaming fags between privet and pebbledash, Church Drive's golden street-lights.

The Curse

'The Charterhouse team were educated gentlemen and undoubted 'swells' when compared to their rough and ready opponents, every man of whom has inherited the primaeval curse and has to earn his bread by the sweat of his brow.' (Athletics News, *reporting Blackburn Olympic's 4-0 F.A. Cup semi-final victory over Old Carthusians on March 17th, 1883.*)

Who are they, these sons of drawl that dare defy their Maker?
Their mouths of violence drip with scorn, their eyes abase and
lay their servants low. Thighs like cedars, torsos cragged from
Sion. Hands of white kid. Hair like spun gold. Beards oiled with
musk from Jezebel's breasts, Bathsheba's polecat balsam. Who
freed them from the Curse? Who lit the light, their brands and
torches, snapped the Garden's chains? O workhouse Christ,
broke and bled on Pilate's looms, I faithful toil in righteous dark
for just dessarts of coin. Look how the Serpent frolics! Merciful
God, let emnitie increase, that we might stamp upon their heads,
and yet not bruise our heels.

Pindaric Ode to Corinth

Blackburn Rovers 1-8 Corinthian (15th December, 1884, Leamington Street, Blackburn). Corinthian: M.J. Rendall, A. Watson, W.F. Beardshaw, A. Amos, C. Holden-White, F.E. Saunders, F.W Pawson, B.W. Spilsbury, Dr. J. S. Miller, W.N. Cobbold, T. Lindley. Rovers: Lofthouse, McIntyre, Beverly, Edwards, Suter, Forrest, Douglas, Sowerbutts, Brown, Avery, Hargreaves.

Imperious Jesus, whose dazzling Palestinian blood
chrismed from cross and blazed to light red-coat colonia
and wine-dark scarlet seas, send seraphs and cherubim,
choriambic Kings of Israel and Judah, to swell the stands
with song: laud and be-laurel the octo-magnificent
Isthmian masters of game. Lindley and Miller, Spilsbury,
Pawson, Cobbold and tar-brushed Amos, contempt
and humbling lucred louts of Lancaster's aspirant blood.

Unread hands from mine and mill, pound-pocketing Scots,
serfs to swanking self-made boors; hard-faced hackers
proud of price, ignoble nobblers of noble Queens –
ludere causa ludendi – laid low and lorded
on Leamington's soot-black, sordid sward.
Lindley of Caius and the Midland Circuit, Doc Miller
and Spillers of Great Divide; eight golden goals to one,
shamsters shamed with gentil virtue: play up, and play the game.

Suter stymied by English stone
Longshanks Saunders crowned on Scone,
Jimmy Doug and Hughie Mac
skinned by 'Nuts' from front to back.
The pros undone, their agents rage,
the gents receive the *Green Un's* praise;
music and manners, speed and grace,
Victoria's kind and conquering race –
play up Corinth and play the game
for game's delight, immortal name.

Christ Aryan and Anglican, whose proud invigorate
wood-worker's blood foamed fierce and Kingly
from marrow of clean-bred bones, come surfing scuds
of trumping heaven, praise rain on burnished Corinth.
Diligent of drill, muscular of matric, lungs bugling
with Psalms, they drum the headstrong turf like Pytchley,
hurtling hurdles of hobnail and headbutt, of elbow oblivious
and pit-bottom rating in gallop to goal and glory.

Clogs clatter on flash-lit cobbles, the drenched streets
rinse and shine. At Ewood and Darwen, crowns spangle
the turf like stars nightfallen wild Atlantic's blue
depression skies. Fracas and scramble, each fisticuffed cove
for himself, grasping team-mates trampled down to seize
his thirty pieces: once Jock with his pipe and fireside dram,
at rest from twelve-hour fury of forge – there is honour in that:
in the rust-bit blade of dissembling Suter, Douglas's
                                        cobwebbed saws?

Out-of-pocket guarantee
in lieu of cash performance fee,
for Corinth plays in Exchange Street –
invoice, dividend, receipt.
Unlike crippled Fergus Suter
riveting plate till the shipyard hooter
blares, and the working day relents
and limps to his cockroach tenement,
where even a dram can't ease the pain:
play up Corinth, play the game.

Non licet omnibus adire Corinthum

There is no fixed rule defining a member's qualifications,
but there is an unwritten law confining election to Old
Public School Boys or members of a university.
  – B.O. Corbett, Thame Grammar School, Oriel College,
           Corinthian F.C. & England.

The myriad viands of Golden Mile
scanted their idiote palates – professing
codfish-in-batter and chipped-potatoes,
the athletes had swaggered off tiddly-om-pom,
to gorge on their monkey-gland, magneton
soul-food, muscled-up pygmies dining to giants,
pot-bellied on Dublin porter.
                                        At length,
crisp linen, the Palatine Hotel;
oysters off the half-shell, '61 Cliquot.
The porne at table flirting with Cunners;
int you a size, Sir. Cunliffe sportive;
I suppose I am, my dear – a sly glance
at Charlie – *well, all the girls say so.*
Oakers rolling his eyes, Joe looking down
at his shellfish; the fellowship falling about.
A warm un an all. Cunners raising his eyebrows
and turning away, tapping the ash
from his cigar; a dozen Campaspes
in Mayfair apartments, unnumbered
country house hetairai.
                                  Players banging
the plate glass window, ruddy as rustics –
Tower Ballroom to grab some birds.
The gentlemen rose and adjusted their cummerbunds,
Oakers and Joe retiring. There was drinking,
then dancing, Cunners and Charlie, Tinsley Lindley,
stripping the silks of champagne showgirls
in five-guinea suites at the Grand Hotel:

straight-shot Steve and Nudger Needham,
dropping five-bob bloomers and rusty arseholes
against the stanchions of the Central Pier.

The Scottish Game

'Are you all Englishmen?'
'Yes Sir.'
'Then I have very much pleasure in presenting you with the ball.
You have played a very good game and I hope you win the Cup.'

Exchange between referee Major A.F. Marindin (Eton & the Royal Military Academy) and the eleven Englishmen of West Bromwich Albion, who had just beaten Preston North End 3-1 in the semi-final of the 1886-87 F.A. Cup competition. The Preston side contained several working-class Scotsmen whose commitment to getting paid and 'combination play' were key elements in transforming the public-school-dominated English game, with its bullies and expense account 'amateurism'.

i. Hampden Tiki-Taka

Wallace and Bruce   tossing cabers
with Darnley and Bothwell   John Broon rampant
    Monarch of the Glen   cradling the bag
jings!   blowing his chanter   Blair
    Nick Fairburn   and Sheena Easton
going hammer and tongs   with Crosspatch Geordies
    Jimmy Boyle   Arthur   and DC Thomson
v. Wrexham   Oswestry   Aston Villa
    Westminster Old Boys   Blackburn Olympic
and finally   Rovers   at Kennington Oval
    where Watt   finds Smith   to Allan
and   CHRISTIE!   congratulate manly handshakes only
    no beastliness   under ye tartan blankets
Cerne Abbas Etonians   might bully and barge   BUT
    Suter & Douglas   in cotton   combine
feeding   BROWN!   & FORREST!
    Glenmorangie and Ginger   Tunnock's coconut snowballs
with Shanks and Souness   Slim Jim Baxter
    Xavi Hernández   and Nicola Sturgeon   YES!

ii. The Scottish Professors

Joe Smith took a third from Keble; matric
was always a bugbear. The History School;
little Latin, less Greek; joined Dunn at Ludgrove,
preparing boys for Eton – play soccer,
love God and hate Harrow.
                                        James Lang
swapped the rivet and plate of Clyde for a no-work
job in a Sheffield cutler's. He read *Bell's Life*
and turned-out for Wednesday.
                                        Fergus Suter
downed tools and took Walsh's brown envelope;
enticed to Turton for a ton; boots nailed
and plated, spiked with gutta percha.
                                        Jack Ross
banked the Cotton Kings' coin. *Slater.* Twelve months
to roof a Deepdale shithouse.
                                        Inglis, Douglas
McIntyre, Graham & Strachan: guns for hire.
     'Football player wanted for a club
in Northeast Lancashire. To a really good man
who can teach well, liberal wages will be given.'
(Advertisement in the Scotsman, *October, 1882.)*
     And what did they profess? Pass-and-move,
the love of money; that poverty is the root of all evil.

iii. The Ballad of Jack Ross

Ross	*You're not a patch on your brother, are you?*
P.M. Walters	*[crestfallen] No, I suppose not.*
Ross	*You'd be no use at all if it wasn't for him. In fact,*
	there's only one better back than A.M.
P.M. Walters	*Who?*
Ross	*Me.*

Jack Ross was born on Gorgie Road
in a rat-hole tenement,
water running down the walls
three-months arreared of rent.

Young Jack came out kicking,
some say he never stopped,
from Bernard's Well to the Dancing Club
he tripped and hacked and chopped.

Fleet as a racing snap-dog,
game as a scarred Blue Paul,
he dogged the pitch from box-to-box
in rush and ruck and maul.

Sharp as a border sheepdog,
wise as a hoar deerhound,
he strode the field and ran the game
for Saturday's sneaking pound.

King Cotton came a-calling,
and trebled his backhand cash;
Jack headed South to terrorise
those milksop Sassenachs.

His teeth were green as spat catarrh
and through them clenched he'd hiss
threats and murder at his foes
till their knickers streaked with piss.

He hobbled Billy Bassett,
snapped James Brown like a stick,
kicked Nevill Cobbold in the nuts
and tenderised his dick.

No forward could get past him,
he smashed down everyone,
but Sudell would not pay his worth –
so he signed for Everton.

But Anfield's up-front hundred pounds
bought only a single season,
for a hundred more from sour Sudell
helped loyal Jack see reason.

But Jack was not the man he was –
there was something on his chest
and after every match a coughing-fit
left blood streaked down his vest.

Sudell sent him to Madeira
that he might recuperate
and get back to his blinding best –
and staunch the bleeding from the gate.

But Gorgie's blight had rotted deep
and Jack was too far gone;
he died in his Fishwick terrace
at the age of thirty-one.

Ten thousand lined the pouring streets
to see Jack's grand cortege,
and bowed their dripping, hatless heads
as the mournful piper played.

And every mill-hand's running dog
threw back its head and howled
at the tumbril's stately passage
to St. Stephen's clay-gouged goal.

And the curtains closed on Fishwick's streets,
the blinds on Gorgie Road
and Jock devoured by England's earth,
into Hell enrolled.

And the curtains closed at Tynecastle,
and closed on Deepdale's stage,
where ten thousand mill-hands, Bill Sudell,
roared applause – and wage.

Their lucred approbation
rocked Satan's fiery gaol
and raptured Gorgie's ghostly-gun
back to Preston's golden dale.

Where sovereigns and brown envelopes
were pressed in pallid palm –
'Encore, Jack! Take a bow, son!
In our grief, you were our balm.'

iv. 'Who do you think you are lad, – '

When they talk of Matthews and Pele
Of Laughton and Finney and James
Like a whisky in your belly
He will glow amongst those names.
  (Ronnie Hilton, 'The Ballad of Billy Bremner')

    Red socks   so there'll be no clash of colours
made redder   wee Bertie's six-studs
    big Mick's shin-bone   wee Billy
after him with a hatchet   couldn't get near him

    wee Jimmy   twisting Cooper's blood
big Norman   *break his fucking legs*
    couldn't get near him

    wee Billy flew in   two-foot head-butt elbows flailing
wee Jimmy   jinking away

    wee Bertie   big Georgie   howling mad Murdoch
passing through them   in tessellate triangles
    Parkhead tiki-taka   never mind the date
just remember the year

    feeding time   and the Lions were hungry   BUT
big Norman on a loose ball   slipped in wee Billy
    pick that out   you cocky Jock cunts
punching the air   those wrong
    red socks   big Mick   big Jack
Norman bites-your-legs   white socks drenched   RED
    mist descending

    for the millionth time   wee Jimmy
sat Cooper on his arse   Billy hit him like a dray-truck
    red socks   red mouths
two knife-faced gingas   swinging straight razors

          to no end
big John Sprake-smash   howling mad Murdoch
        give best   wee Billy
to the Lions of Lisbon   best
        to wee Bertie   and Quality Street

        put on swapped hoops
and wear with pride   BUT   those wrong red socks
        Tibbut and Guthrie   with Sugden going through
Speed or Clarke or Clegg   *get down*
        Tibbut sent off   fat twat wants milking
red socks   shirt off   V-signs   wankers
        wee Billy   red Kev
going hammer and tongs   for Sir Stan and big Ted
        at the Empire Stadium   Wembley

The Zulus

Rosa Parks and Jim Forrest at the back of the bus,
players picking cotton in the Middlesex outfield.
Juleps in the Long Room, W.G., Kinnaird;
Bill Beldham breaking gent's apartheid, dying
for a pint: Grace swooning – *I do declare.*
Isandlwana; gentlemen, players – butchered
by Cetshwayo's impi. Without distinction.
Gandhi burning his passbook, Dolly slammed
to Seal Island by the Rugby Football Union.
Twenty thousand assegais crossing
the White Umfolozi; a thousand wailing widows,
five thousand snot-nosed kids.
Jack to the rescue,
big white Hunter; showboat minstrel, Swanee river –
Sunday Night at the London Palladium.
Or, Victoria Ground, Worsborough Common,
twin Mansions of Rastafari; the burnt-cork pros
of Sheffield's Zulu v. the pit-muck miners
of the Barnsley Select. Each man black
as the Ace of Spades, dusky as Darkie Wharton,
mocha-choca Minah Bird. *Hey Joe, won't you
give it a go?* Zulus rattling cowhide shields
and passing round the bucket. *Lodda good work
for charidee.* Oversized red-coats on skinny
intanga. Strange constellations, skeleton dreams;
mammy's waiting and praying for me.
Eleven coin-counting music hall rogues,
plumed in ostrich, rattling beads. Hunter
as war-chief Dabulamanzi, pot-bellied Buttery,
Cetshwayo himself. They were having a laugh;
Jiggleumbendo, Oomitingy, Nina Baden Semper.
But after the clowning, a game was played.
Six-nil to the victors of Isandlwana, relief

to the Poor Law's waifs and strays. To the impi,
the spoils; say, a quid to cover expenses,
nosebag and rinse in the tent at full-time.
        The Sheffield F.A. pronounced its anathema;
the Zulus were exiled to their Blackburn bantustan
and the widows to the workhouse – no outdoor relief.
'Jack, play for pleasure, and the good of the game.
Earn from your trade and keep your good name' –
Dabulamanzi, three-sheets-to-the-wind
at Worsborough Miners' Welfare, clog-dancing
for nobbins. Streaked like a zebra.
Weel-about and turn-about and do jis so,
ebry time I weel-about, I jump Jim Crow.

Park Estate Garrincha

Joy of Pau Grande, Joy of Mage,
Joy of Brazil, Joy of the World.

From opposite the Spar, far side of Park Estate.
You knew his type – *urchin* – always smudged
and sooty, permanent sleep-tousled hair;
wore Winfield pumps and market jeans, cast-off shirts
and a skinny-rib Parka. Cadged tabs, pinched Polos;
made Tarzan calls and monkey noises, slapped kisses
on grossed-out, shrieking girls. Played football,
could dribble better than Best, but couldn't get up
in the mornings, get himself a pair of boots –
resist going through pockets in the changing rooms.
Grew seamless to adulthood in the social's comfy rut,
a thirty-year run to a premature funeral
in a booze-fuzzed haze of front room fag-smoke
and afternoon TV, routinely enlivened by family dysfunction:
vigilantes at the door for the smacked-up son,
boyfriend battering the pregnant daughter,
three months here-and-there for burglary or receiving.
They found him stiff on the sofa, Jerry Springer on TV.
At his wake we got drunk with his brothers, and agreed
he would have made it, if only he'd got the breaks –
a bandy-legged genius from the council house favela,
Joy of Park Estate, Joy of Kirkby Rec,
Joy of the Ponty Road End, Joy of the World.

Enganche

G.O. Smith, Roker Park, 18th February, 1899.

Sole gent in a team of players – G.C. Vassell
withdrew to captain the Varsity,
Villa's Athersmith replacing. Thirteen-two,
still a record. He bagged four 'from the scrimmage'
and set-up the inside forwards; a brace
for Bloomer, and Settle, a hat-trick.
He even played Athersmith in from left wing.
And 'missed' a penalty, passed-back to the goalie
in the true Corinthian spirit. Daft bugger;
he could've gone nap, or at least stepped aside
to give Bloomer *his* hat-trick. The game more-so
than the winning. He learned it in whites
as much as in Cloisters, at Palace, or at Queens.
Clean-boned, clear-eyed, ascetic, aesthetic,
projecting a stern, almost feminine, rectitude –
Stonyhurst Hopkins or Thomas Street Yeats.
Awaiting the whistle in Jermyn bespoke,
hands loitering deep in nonchalant pockets,
he shares a quip with J.C. Oakley, quotes Horace
with C.B. Fry – banters on baseball
with Bloomer. Drifting between the lines,
linking it all together. Lean as a whipcord.

Jubilate Messi

'For there is a note added to the scale, which the Lord hath made fuller, stronger and more glorious.' (Christopher Smart, Jubilate Agno)

I will rejoice in Lionel Andrés Messi; for he leaps before the Lord like David, and his joy is uncovered: *Let the rain streak bright in the flaring floodlights, Empire's phosphorescent rainbow arching like a cat.*

For he is brave and boyish, with the dark eyes of the pit-dog and the shy mouth of the wolf : *Let him shear the sheep of the bloody devil, pluck the condors of Falange.*

For the cunning Right Hand and gloried Left Foot are but gifts from the finger of God: *Let left triumph over right, the shin-snapping lunges of Goikoetxea and Ramos, the death-dives of Videla.*

For cocaine and cortisone, Diego's duende, Thatcher and Shilton's woes: *Let Castro and Kirchner join in applause for Azteka's avenging viveza.*

For Jack flies over Stanley, Belgrano is coffined at sea: *Let Butcher and Beardsley, Fenwick and Reid be ruthless as Rattín, savage as Samuel, brutal as Batista.*

For he dusts down and demurs not, nor will he fall to foul or faking: *Let them be honest as the horse and humble as the ass.*

For he has the grace of Garrincha and the guts of Gascoigne; Zola's zest, the balance of Best, and Bergkamp's balmy touch: *Let Der Bomber give praise, and Henry's heart, leap like the lenten roe.*

For Garrincha lies dead in his drunkard's grave, Best slaughtered, Gazza mortal: *Let maté be prepared and neapolitan schnitzel, Milanello's pasta e pollo.*

For Guevara fought with Simba in Congo, El Proceso v. Task Force and those disappeared: *Let Cuito Cuanavale live long in the song, how the FAR pulled the teeth of Die Groot Krokodil.*

For though Sunyol is murdered and Guernica plaint, Galtieri and gauleiters – dead: *Let the cloud-crested noontide soar albiceleste, eventide crimsoned and blue.*

For the lepers shall inherit the mower-striped Earth: *Let the grass spurt green in the urchinned precincts, the playgrounds plunge with boys.*

For Alves knows his duty and gives him the ball: *Let Andrés and Xavi and Pedro attend, Sorín, Saviola, Juan Román Riquelme.*

For Balons and titles are but nets of the Tempter: *Let the spirit flow with joy.*

For he spurts from the butchers like blood-jet, fearless as Fangio, fierce as Gardel: *Let the bobbles and rebounds fall to his fast feet forever.*

Notes

Tohuwabohu – the title is a transliteration of the Hebrew words translated as 'without form and void' in the King James Version of Genesis 1:2. This poem narrates the creation of football at the beginning of time via a conflation of the Hebrew and Orphic creation myths. The Promethean figure 'Pramanath' seizes the ball from God and brings the game to Earth.

Football at Crowe Street, 1721 – the poem is based on the eponymous engraving and locates the elusive 'Crowe Street' at Smithfield, London; the action takes place during Bartholomew Fair and the game's rolling maul starts at St. Bartholomew's Church and ends at Clerkenwell Gate. 'Chanticleer' is a folk name for a cockerel; 'Bent Bob' & the 'Sour Kraut King' are Prime Minister Robert Walpole and King George I; 'Jock Chartres' is Colonel Francis Charteris, the dissolute Scottish rake who made Sally-from-our-Alley' (Sally Salisbury, the most celebrated whore of the period) his mistress until he tired of her when she turned fourteen.

In Cloisters – 'Deo dante dedi' ('God giving, I gave' – the motto of Charter-house School). The various forms of football played at Charterhouse (the Cloister and Green games, including runabout, shootabout and puntabout, played a key role in the emergence and definition of Association Football in the mid-1800s. In this poem the improvised public-school game is juxtaposed with vernacular forms of football and related ball games played by kids on South Kirkby's Wimpey Estate in the 1970s.

Pindaric Ode to Corinth – 'Corinth' is Corinthian F.C., the elite gentleman-amateur team of public schoolboys and Oxbridge graduates, considered the finest football team in the country until the rise of the professional game in the 1880s proved otherwise. The victory Corinthian achieved over Blackburn Rovers in the game commemorated in this poem was their last hurrah. Blackburn were the F.A. Cup holders and widely regarded as the best team in Britain, having defeated the elite Scottish amateur side Queen's Park (motto, 'ludere causa ludendi', 'to play for the sake of playing') in the final. Corinth arranged the friendly match against Blackburn to avenge the humiliation inflicted on their class by a team of working men. 'Leamington' Road was the home of Blackburn Rovers in the 1880s. Fergus Suter, Jimmy Douglas and Hughie MacIntyre were imported Scottish, under-the-table professionals (professionalism was not sanctioned by the F.A. until 1885), much despised by the gentlemen.

Non licet omnibus adire Corinthum – after the F.A. authorised professionalism in 1885, professionals and amateurs were able to play together in the same team, including the English national team, which by the 1890s comprised a mixture of working-class professionals from teams such as Preston North End, Aston Villa and Sheffield United, and patrician amateurs, most of whom were selected from Corinthian F.C. Boundaries between gentleman and player began to relax, although, as this imagined night out in Blackpool after an international in the North-West seems to assert, it is hard to imagine two such alien and antagonistic cultures ever becoming fully integrated. 'Idiote' and 'athlete' were C.B. Fry's (Repton, Oxford, Corinthian, England) characterisation of the gentleman amateur and the professional, respectively. 'Cunners' is Robert Cunliffe Gosling, Old Etonians, Corinthian and England and the 'richest man ever to play football in England'; 'Oakers' is J.C. Oakley, Old Carthusians, Corinthian and England; 'Joe' is G.O. Smith, Old Carthusians, Corinthian and England – and Oakers' great friend and colleague at Ludgrove School. 'Charlie' is Charles Wreford Brown, Old Carthusians, Corinthian and England, coiner of the neologism 'soccer'. Dr. Tinsley Lindley played for Corinthian, Nottingham Forest, Notts County, Crusaders, Swifts, Preston North-End and England. 'Steve' Bloomer was a blacksmith who became a professional footballer with Derby County, Middlesbrough & England. Ernest 'Nudger' Needham was a miner who became a professional footballer with Sheffield United and England. 'Non licet omnibus adire Corinthum' is a maxim of Horace, a writer much loved by the classicist C.B. Fry, which literally translates, 'not everyone may go to Corinth'.

The Scottish Game – 'the Scottish Game' was the name given to passing football – or 'combination play' – in England in the late 19th century. English football had been based on individual dribbling, 'bullies' and scrimmages. The example of Scottish amateurs Queens Park and the arrival of Scottish professionals to the English game brought pass-and-move into the English game and changed our football permanently and for the better.

Hampden Tiki-Taka – the 1884 F.A. Cup Final between Blackburn Rovers and Queen's Park is at the heart of this poem. 'Tiki-taka' is the name given to the intricate passing football perfected by Barcelona F.C. under Pep Guardiola, 2008-2012. 'The Scottish Game' was an early precursor of the style.

The Scottish Professors – 'Joe Smith'; see note to 'Non licet omnibus adire Corinthum', above. 'Dunn', A.T.B. Dunn, Old Etonians, Corinthian & England, founder and Headmaster of Ludgrove Preparatory School. Glasgow's Fergus Suter was an under-the-table professional at Darwen, but was lured across town to Blackburn Rovers by a better offer from mill owner John Boothman, the financial power behind the club; 'Jack Ross', Nicholas John Ross, Hearts, Preston North End, Everton & Scotland, the Duncan Edwards—or Roy Keane—of his day, was ostensibly a slater; John Inglis, Jimmy Douglas and Hughie McIntyre were three other 'Scottish professors' who played for Blackburn Rovers in the 1884 Cup Final. Tommy Strachan played for Blackburn in the 1886 final & Ayr's Johnny Graham played for Preston in 1888.

The Ballad of Jack Ross – Jack Ross, see note, above. 'Dancing Club' – the first incarnation of Heart of Midlothian F.C.; a 'snap-dog' is a whippet; a 'Blue Paul' is a legendary pitbull-type dog; 'Sudell' is Bill Sudell, the impresario behind the rise of Preston North-End in the 1880s.

'Who do you think you are, lad—' – in which the European Cup semi-final second leg between Glasgow Celtic and Leeds United (15th April, 1970, 2-1 to Celtic) merges with the fifth round F.A. Cup tie between Manchester United and Tottenham Hotspur (Easter 1969, St. Helens' County Secondary Modern

School, Barnsley, 1-2 to Tottenham) around the figure of Billy Bremner. Bertie Auld, Mick Jones, Jimmy Johnstone, Terry Cooper, Norman Hunter, Georgie Connelly, Bobby Murdoch, Jack Charlton, John Hughes and Gary Sprake are the other players name-checked. 'Quality Street' was the name given to the Celtic youth system which was a production line of outstanding home-grown players. 'Tibbut', 'Guthrie', 'Speed', 'Clarke' & 'Clegg' are players from the Manchester United v. Tottenham cup-tie; 'Sugden' was a slightly balding Bobby Charlton; 'red Kev' is Liverpool's Kevin Keegan, sent off along with Bremner for fighting during the 1974 Charity Shield in front of patrician luminaries Ted Croker of the Football League and Sir Stanley Rous of the Football Association.

The Zulus – in 1879, noted Sheffield footballer Jack Hunter formed a touring football team called the Zulus in order to raise money for the widows of the British soldiers killed at Isandlwana. In a precursor of the later 'minstrel' shows, the Zulus wore all-black kit, darkened their skins with burnt-cork, decorated their uniforms with feathers and beads and adopted Zulu names. The grandees of the Sheffield Football Association, led by Charles Clegg, a prosperous local solicitor and temperance campaigner, were profoundly antagonistic to the Zulus, who they believed were bringing the game into disrepute not only by the undignified burlesque of their performance and the drinking and roister that attended their matches, but by their thinly-veiled professionalism. Accordingly, the Zulus were banned from playing in the jurisdiction of the Sheffield F.A. Many of the Zulus, including Hunter himself, were forced to move to Lancashire to earn a living from football, where they ultimately played a key role in forcing the patricians of the FA to end their discrimination against working-class professionals. Of course, even after professionalism was accepted, working-class footballers had to endure humiliations. In 1885, Blackburn Rovers' Jim Forrest was forced to wear a different coloured shirt (his club shirt) to his public school, amateur team-mates when he was the only professional in the England team that represented England against a Scotland XI made up entirely of amateurs from the Queen's Park club. Bill Beldham was an early 'player' (as opposed to gentleman) in the cricketing world and received similar prejudice to that received by James Forrest. Basil 'Dolly' D'Oliveira was an English cricketer of 'Cape Coloured' extraction dropped by the English selectors from their 1968 tour of South Africa so as not to offend the Government of apartheid South Africa; 'Seal Island' is Robben Island, where Nelson Mandela and other political prisoners were incarcerated by successive apartheid regimes. The 'White Umfolozi' is a South African river; 'Victoria Ground, Worsborough Common', the venue of a charity match between the Zulus and a Barnsley XI; Arthur 'Darkie' Wharton was probably England's first black professional footballer, playing for a range of sides including Preston North-End, Sheffield United and Rotherham; 'Minah Bird' was a Nigerian model and actress of the 1970s, often referred to as 'dusky' by the tabloid press, as was Trinidadian actress 'Nina Baden Semper'. An allusion to LaBelle's 'Lady Marmalade' is also in there somewhere.

Park Estate Garrincha – Garrincha '(Little Bird') – Manuel Francisco dos Santos, the most naturally talented Brazilian footballer of the 1950s and 1960s. Uneducated, unworldly and hedonistic, Garrincha was grievously exploited during his career and died an impoverished alcoholic, aged only 49. His gravestone in his hometown of Pau Grande is inscribed, 'Garrincha, Joy of Pau Grande, Joy of Mage, Joy of Brazil, Joy of the World'.

Enganche – this homage to Gilbert Oswald 'Joe' Smith takes as its starting point England's record 13-2 victory over Ireland in 1899, in which Smith was the sole amateur in a team of professionals. In a ten-year career, Smith played for Old Carthusians, Oxford University, the Casuals, Corinthian F.C. and England. He also played first class cricket for Oxford University and Surrey. Smith excelled in what was effectively the 'false nine' or 'enganche' (literally 'hook') position, scoring prolifically (132 in 137 appearances for Corinthian F.C.) and laying on as many as he scored. Although very much a gentleman amateur, Smith did not condescend to his working-class, professional team mates (unlike so many of his contemporaries) and was a man without petty pride. A schoolmaster at Ludgrove School in Cockfosters, Smith retired from football in 1902, aged 31. Scholars of the game still regard Smith as one of the best English footballers of all time. Steve 'Bloomer' of Derby County, Joe's strike partner for England, also played baseball for Derby.

Jubilate Messi – the poem is associative. I can't think of Messi without thinking of Maradona and Argentina, I can't think of Argentina without thinking of the Falklands, of Maradona without thinking of the Azteca in 1986 and his later friendship with Castro, of Castro without ... you get the idea. There's too much in the poem to give a comprehensive account, but, King David leapt before the Lord in 2 Samuel 6; the Empire Stadium's arch was lit in Barcelona's colours after the 2011 Champions League final; 'condors of Falange' refers to the Nazi Condor legion, which the Real Madrid-supporting Generalissimo Franco directed to bomb the people of Catalunya and Euskal Herria in the 1930s; Athletic Bilbao's Andoni Goikoetxea infamously broke Maradona's ankle in 1983; Sergio 'Ramos' has not yet succeeded in breaking Messi's, despite twelve years of trying. Jorge 'Videla' was the Fascist President of Argentina from 1979-1981. He would 'disappear' dissidents by the simple expedient of having his airforce fly them over the Atlantic and throw them in the ocean. 'Der Bomber' is German striker Gerd Müller, 'Henry' is Messi's former team-mate Thierry; 'mate' and 'neopolitan schnitzel' are Messi's favourite drink and food respectively; the 'Simba' rebellion was launched against Mobutu Sese Seko's CIA backed reactionaries in 1964, by forces loyal to the assassinated former President Patrice Lumumba; 'El Proceso' was the name given to the Argentinian military dictatorship, 1976-1983; at the battle of 'Cuito Canavale' in Namibia in 1989, the Cuban *Fuerzas Armadas Revolucionarias* ('FAR') combined with SWAPO to decisively defeat and force back invading South African forces, thus thwarting the hegemonic ambitions of apartheid Prime Minister Piet Botha, 'Die Groot Krokodil'. Josep 'Sunyol' i Garriga, a left-wing Catalan nationalist and President of A.F.C. Barcelona, was kidnapped and murdered by Francoists in 1936. The 'albiceleste' is the Argentinian national football team. 'Lepers' is the nickname of Newell's Old Boys, the football team Lionel Messi supported as a boy in his home town of Rosario.